The 1ˢᵗ Three Years of Dance

Teaching Tips, Monthly Lesson Plans, and Syllabi
for Successful Dance Classes

By Gina Evans

Terry, Noelle, and Frank, thank you for your friendship, support, and love.

The 1ˢᵗ Three Years of Dance

*Teaching Tips, Monthly Lesson Plans, and Syllabi
for Successful Dance Classes*

Introduction

After over 20 years of teaching I realized teaching for young dancers is as much talent and training as it is a formula. I am a naturally good teacher, but I was going into class after class, day after day, year after year, without an overall plan. I was continually spending time developing classes each month and each year.

Once I opened my own studio, I realized the case was the same for everyone. I hired good teachers, but they too were trying to reinvent the wheel year after year. This was costing them time and me money. It also caused for a lot of classes to get stale, and we would lose students because they would get bored or parents would not see progress. You need change in the class month to month and between the different levels. This will show the untrained eye of parents that dance education is a process, and a student cannot learn it all in one year. We also had problems with multiple teachers, that when a child would switch teachers mid-year or even in their 2nd or 3rd year of dance, they would not have equal knowledge as the other students in the class. They would not be better or worse than the other students, just have different knowledge. This took time to get the class back on the same page.

I have taken my years of experience and developed a common base around which all my teachers can build their classrooms. Giving students an equal, strong dance education in their early years will allow classes in later years to have room for students' talents, education, and creativity to thrive.

Chapter One
Teaching Tips

Keep it Moving

This statement explains itself. You lose children's attention, lose control of the class, and you may lose a student because of boredom. Do not spend too much time on any one activity. Have your music in a playlist so you do not have to change a CD or find a song to use. Have any props ready to use. And do not choreograph dances during class time.

Repetition can be Different

Dance skills are learned through repetition, which can become very boring to small (and sometimes older) children. You may hear parents say things like, "Susie's class is too easy. I want her moved up to the next level," or, "Anna has already learned how to dance, so we are going to try soccer." This is all because of the repetition needed to learn dance. Students and parents do not understand that you always need the basics and will be improving on them your entire dance career. Adding different qualities and visual references to movement can enhance learning. Change music and the pace of the movement. Change center work to across the floor. Give visual references, such as dancing on a cloud or being as loud as an elephant. Even when using the same lesson plan all month you can (and need to) make changes.

Dance = Fun

Young children are there for fun and the love of movement. Parents want their children to enjoy the class over anything else. The hard work and training can come in later years. You need to be the best, coolest, most amazing thing in the room. You need to hold their attention by being FUN. Remember we do not want students to get bored or distracted. Do not be afraid to be silly, goofy, or funny. Keep your energy up!

Dancing in Words

Visuals are very important when teaching younger children. You want to use visuals to explain specific steps, i.e.: point your toes = princess feet, flexed feet = frog feet. To keep their heads up, tell them they are wearing a crown; rond de jambe = drawing circles on the floor. You want them to use expression, too. Have them try a step and make it happy, sad, mad, etc. Pretend to be someone or something; have them try a step as a princess, a witch, a clown, an elephant, etc. Change the texture of the movement—dance on a cloud, dance in thick yogurt, or dance on fire.

If There Isn't a Choice, Don't Ask a Question

If you say, "don't you want to dance?" You better be ready for the kid to say no. Never ask a question when you do not really want an answer. It is better to say, "Come and dance." Also, do not make promises you cannot keep, such as, "We will play with the scarves next week." The students will remember you said this even if you do not. If you do not have a plan to do it or if you are not going to remember it, then do not say it. A line leader, or going first, is always a problem in class. It can cause arguments and disappointment. Many teachers have different opinions on how to handle this. No one-way is right or wrong, but make your rule, explain your rule, and stick with it all year.

Praise the Good

We want students to model good behavior. This involves the good behavior of other children and of you! Bad behavior is what most children will tend to model, especially if bad behavior is what is getting your attention. Point out who is doing it right so other students follow along. "Grace is pointing her toes, Anna is pointing her toes, Suzie is pointing her toes…" until you get everyone pointing their toes. Be specific to what good behavior is being exhibited; say the student's name and the specific thing he/she is doing well. "Good job" is not specific. You also want to limit negative attention. If a child only hears his/her name because he/she is always doing something wrong, he/she will quit listening. Another trick is to praise what you want to see. If students are not keeping their hands to themselves, do not jump right to, "Everyone needs to keep their hands to themselves." Instead say, "I love how everyone is keeping their hands to themselves." This will work with all kinds of behaviors—try it!

Waiting can be Difficult

Sometimes taking turns is needed, but waiting can be difficult (especially in a big class). When students get bored with an activity, change to the next one as soon as possible. If you cannot change within the next minute, distract them. You can change the line order so they are standing in different places in the room, or you can change the visuals of the movement. Give the students who are waiting a task. You can have them stand in different dance positions or poses. Have the next student in line pick the pose and everyone holds it until it's the next person's turn.

Build Relationships

To keep students in your class, first they need to have fun, and second they need to build relationships. If they have friends in class they will be more likely to come back. This is the same your relationship to students and their parents. Create share time with the class. If they tell you they are doing something exciting next week, remember it and ask them about it the next time you see them. The same goes with the parents. With parents it is better that they stay in the building (preferably a waiting room—not in the classroom) and talk. If they make friendships with the other parents, they will want their children to continue with the class.

Chapter Two

Introduction to Lesson Plans and Syllabi

There are three levels of syllabi and lessons plans labeled as Petite A, Petite B, and Petite C. These classes are designed for younger students and work well with any combination of students, ages 2 – 7 years old. The syllabi for each level are the end result of that year's training; this is what I expect the dancers to be able to accomplish by the end of the year. There are dance skills listed along with points of focus under each skill. I normally use the French terms for the positions of the arms and feet in ballet. I do not expect a perfect execution of the steps, but for the students to have mastered the major concepts listed with each skill. Under tumbling, since there are many different names for the same skill, I tried to explain the activity in clear terms. There are also additional concepts in italics. These are progressions for the student who may master the skill faster than others. The goal is to keep them from getting bored. Petite A is ballet and tumbling. Petite B is ballet, tumbling, and tap. Petite C is ballet and tap. I have it broken up this way because after years of teaching tap to young, first year students who spent more time sliding around on the floor than dancing, I figured out that they do not have the control or attention span to consistently stay productive on their feet. Plus, the change in curriculum from level to level is a way to show the untrained eye of parents that this is a progressive process; it does not and cannot be learned in one year.

Next there are ten months' worth of lesson plans for each level. For each month in all three levels, in addition to the dance steps, you will see *share time*, *walking into the classroom*, *free dance*, *games*, *monthly dance* and *story time*. These are key components of creating structure in your classroom, building relationships with your students, and adding in a little extra fun.

First, it is important for students to line up at the door and walk in together. This keeps the students out of the classroom so you can finish your last class and/or prepare for your next class. It also gives an official starting procedure to the class and helps them understand that although dance is fun, it is not free playtime.

Before walking into the classroom, I always stand with the students for about a minute at the door to the classroom. This is used as our *share time*. I may ask them specific questions, but usually they already have something to tell me as soon as I get there.

The dance steps contained within each lesson plan build on skills learned in previous lessons (where applicable), and also include skills that they may use in the *monthly dances*. As the students progress, remember to use each step in combination with other steps. For example, the tap lesson plan might say to do flaps, followed by flap ball changes. If your students have already accomplished these skills and are getting bored with the repetition, put them all together in a combination, such as flap, flap, flap ball change, or make them try it while changing directions, traveling across the floor, etc. You constantly want to keep the students engaged.

The *free dance* involves a variety of props, improvisation, and music. These is usually students' favorite part of class, since they get to move around freely and exercise their individual creativity; however, do not let this turn into students running around in circles for 3 minutes. Guide them by giving visuals as well as different types of music and have them dance to show how it makes them feel. The various *games* and *directional songs* are explained in chapter 10.

Each month there is a brief dance to learn, which I have categorized as the *monthly dance*. These are short combinations set to suggested music, but most will fit any pop/children's song. Each dance is about a minute to 90 seconds long. When reading the choreography, you will see "1 s/o 8" under "counts". This is an abbreviation for "1 set of 8 counts". The dances are filled with the skills in the concurrent lesson plan. The purpose is to help the students understand how steps fit together, to learn to remember choreography, and to show their progress to their parents. If you do not have a viewing window, invite the parents in at the end of each month to watch students perform the dance combination. Do not expect the students to be able to do this completely on their own; use verbal cues and hand gestures to help them remember the movements. The students will feel a sense of accomplishment from performing this small, but complete dance.

The *story time* at the end of each class does not have to be anything specific. There are hundreds of children's books about taking dance class or performing on stage. All your students' favorite characters have shown up in dance at one point or another. But they do not have to be about dance either. You can read the fairy tale behind any of the classical ballets. Only spend about 3 – 5 minutes reading at the end of the class. You do not have to finish a book each week.

Remember to familiarize yourself with the lesson plan before the start of the class. Have all your supplies out where you can get to them easily during the transitions, and have the music on a playlist. This does not mean you will not have to think on your feet and make adjustments throughout the class depending on what is working for your students on that particular day; however, being prepared makes the class run more smoothly when you do have to make changes.

Chapter Three

Petite A Syllabus

- Student waits at the door for teacher's instruction to enter classroom
- Understands finding individual place-markers (colors and/or shapes) as instructed
- Walks "like a dancer" whenever changing locations; does not run

Ballet

Center
- Student stands in line with stomach to mirror

Barre
- Student keeps two hands on the barre and is spaced correctly, leaving enough space between themselves and the next student

Across Floor
- Student in place; sits with legs crossed and back to wall
- Student understands taking turns

Body positions with arms in 1st, 2nd, and 3rd
- Feet turned out
- Arms held correctly in each position

Demi plié in 1st, 2nd, and 3rd positions
- Hands on hips
- Heels stay on the ground in demi plié
- Knees push out to sides making a diamond shape

Tendu, front and back, in 1st position with hands on hips
- Slides foot on the ground, lifts heel, and leaves toe on the ground
- Foot completely extended in tendu

Kicks
- Front, side, and back
- Kicks as high as he/she can
- Correct directional placement
- Knees straight and toes pointed

Relevé,

- Pulls fully up onto demi pointe in relevé

Passé,
- Passé is turned out
- Stomach stays facing wall
- *Only toe touches at knee*

Chassé (sideways), with arms in 2nd position
- Arms stay in 2nd position
- Stomach stays facing the front of the room
- Correct foot leads
- *Feet meet in first, do not cross*

Walking on relevé "Ballerina Walks"
- Sideways and/or forward
- Walks across the floor while staying on relevé

Bourrées (sideways)
- Arms rounded in 5th
- Stomach stays facing the front of the room
- Correct foot leads
- Feet meet in 1st, do not cross

Step, passé
- *Stomach stays facing mirror*
- *Only toe touches at knee*
- *Passé is turned out*

Jumps in 1st position
- Jumps together as a class, with music or counts
- Plié in 1st at start and end
- Lands in 1st position
- *Toes pointed and legs straight in the air*

Échappé sauté
- Jumps together as a class, with music or counts
- Plié in 1st at start and end
- Lands in 1st and 2nd positions
- *Toes pointed and legs straight in the air*

Tumbling
- Student sits with legs crossed and back to wall

- Student understands taking turns
- Walks to and from mat; does not, crawl, run, hop, etc.
- Returns to correct spot in line;

Frog jumps
- Starting with hands and feet ground
- Jumping high with arms up and body straight
- *Legs straight and together in the air*
- Landing with hands and feet ground

Jelly/*Pencil* rolls
- Lay across mat on back
- Rolls straight down mat
- Jelly roll arms are by side
- *Pencil rolls arms above head, hands together, elbows straight*
- *Legs straight, toes pointed*

Army drags
- Lay on stomach
- Uses arms and legs to crawl across the mat
- Does not go up on knees

Seal walks
- Stomach on the ground
- Lifts chest up supported by your arms
- Uses arms to walk down the mat

Monkey jumps
- Place both hand on the beam (or a raised mat)
- Jumps feet from one side of beam to the other
- Supports movement with straight arms
- Lands on feet

Camel walks
- Walks on hands and feet
- Keeps knees and elbows straight when walking

Crab/*Table* walks
- Walks on hands and feet with stomach towards the ceiling
- Travels full length of mat
- Crab walk bottom does not touch the ground
- Walks forwards and backwards
- *Table walk – stomach pushed up to ceiling*

Hops on one foot, forward/*backwards*

- *Keeps foot up for full length of mat*
- *Can do with either right or left foot up, not just on one side*

Forward rolls

- Start in bug with head down (chin on chest)
- Rolls straight, keeps head tucked
- *Rolls back onto feet in bug without pushing with hands*

Straddle rolls

- Sit in a straddle position
- Tuck head in and do a forward roll leaving legs in the straddle position
- End in a straddle like you started

Balance beam

- Walks forward and backwards
- Keeps head up and arms straight out to sides
- Balances in passé (knee faces side); *without assistance*
- Balances in arabesque (leg straight and toes pointed; keeps chest up); *without assistance*

Obstacle course

- Follows direction of 3 task in a row

Chapter Four
Lesson Plans and Monthly Dances for Petite A

Line up; Share time
Walk into room

Ballet
Warm-up in center
- Positions in 1st and 2nd
- Demi pliés in 1st and 2nd
- Kicks front

Across Floor
- Ballerina walks on relevé, keeping stomach to front of the room
- Chassés sideways, keeping stomach to front of the room

Center
- Jumps in 1st, then 1st to 2nd

Monthly Dance – "Swinging on a Star" by Bing Crosby
Free Dance – with scarves
Directional Song – "The Hokey Pokey"
Game – Twister Two

Tumbling
Stretching
- Head – sideways, shoulder-to-shoulder, up and down
- Arms – hug, arm circles
- Touch toes from standing

Progressions
- Hop forward on two feet
- Frog jump
- Jelly rolls
- Camel walks

Balance Beam
- Walk forward

Obstacle Course
1st. Balance Beam – walk forward
2nd. Hula-hoops – jump in and out
3rd. Tunnel – crawl forward

Game – Parachute Tag
Story Time

Counts	Steps	Arms
2 s/o 8	Hold	
1 – 6	3 step turn to right (2 counts each)	Arms in 1st
7 & 8		Clap
1 s/o 8	4 step touches (2 counts each)	Arms up over head
	right, left, right, left	moving with feet
1 – 6	3 step turn to right (2 counts each)	Arms in 1st
7 & 8		Clap
1 – 4	Jump to 2nd, close to 1st	Hands on hips
5 – 8		shake head "no"
1 s/o 8	2 pliés 1st	Hands on hips
1 s/o 8	2 tendus from 1st	Hands on hips
1 s/o 8	2 pliés 1st	Hands on hips
1 s/o 8	2 tendus from 1st	Hands on hips
1 – 4	Relevé	Arms in High 5th
5 – 8	Turn around 1 time	

Repeat from 3 step turn and then create an ending pose after last set of 8

Line up; Share time
Walk into room

Ballet
Warm-up in center

- Positions in 1st and 2nd
- Demi pliés in 1st and 2nd
- Tendus front
- Kicks front

Across Floor

- Ballerina walks on relevé
- Chassés sideways
- Hopscotch with place markers – lay place markers on the ground in a hopscotch pattern and have children take turns jumping

Center

- Port de bras – follow teacher as he/she moves through different arm positions

Monthly Dance – "You've Got a Friend in Me" by Randy Newman
Free Dance – with maracas
Directional Song – "Head, Shoulders, Knees, and Toes"
Game – Parachute Tag

Tumbling
Stretching

- Head – sideways, shoulder-to-shoulder, up and down, circle
- Arms – hug, arm circles, reaches right and left
- Touch toes from standing

Progressions

- Hops forward on two feet
- Frog jumps
- Jelly rolls
- Crab walks

Balance Beam

- Walk backwards

Obstacle Course

1st. Balance Beam – walk backwards
2nd. Cones – walk around them on toes
3rd. Trampoline – jump 10 times

Game – "Miss Gina" Says
Story Time

Counts	Steps	Arms
20 counts	Hold	
2 s/o 8	Ballerina walks forward	Arms up in high 5th
1 s/o 8	4 chassés to right side	Arms out to sides
1 s/o 8	4 chassés to left side	Arms out to sides
2 s/o 8	Ballerina walks backward	Arms up in high 5th
2 s/o 8	Jump to 2nd, close to 1st	
	(4 counts, 4 times)	Hands on hips
2 s/o 8	Ballerina walks forward	Arms up in high 5th
1 s/o 8	4 chassés to right side	Arms out to sides
1 s/o 8	4 chassés to left side	Arms out to sides
2 s/o 8	Ballerina walks backward	Arms up in high 5th
1 – 4	Jump to 2^{nd,} close to 1st	Hands on hips
5 – 8	Jump to 2nd and hold	Hands on hips
1 s/o 8 + 4	3 pliés in 2nd	Hands on hips
5 – 8	Jump to 1st	Hands on hips
1 – 4	Tendu to the side with right foot, close 1st	Hands on hips
5 – 8	Tendu to the side with left foot, close 1st	Hands on hips
1 – 4	Tendu to the side with right foot, close 1st	Hands on hips
5 – 8		Point to self, then
		out to audience

Line up; Share time
Walk into room

Ballet
Warm-up in center
- Positions in 1st and 2nd
- Demi pliés in 1st and 2nd
- Tendus front
- Kicks front

Across Floor
- Ballerina walks on relevé, keeping stomach to front of the room
- Chassés sideways, keeping stomach to front of the room
- Turns

Center
- Port de bras
- Jumps in 1st, then 1st to 2nd

Monthly Dance – "Good Ship Lollipop" by Shirley Temple
Free Dance – with ribbons
Directional Song – "London Bridge is Falling Down"
Game – "Miss Gina" Says

Tumbling
Stretching
- Head – sideways, shoulder-to-shoulder, up and down, circle
- Arms – hug, arm circles, reaches right and left
- Butterfly

Progressions
- Hop backwards on two feet
- Frog jumps
- Log rolls
- Crab walks

Balance Beam
- Walk sideways

Obstacle Course
1st. Balance Beam – walk sideways
2nd. On a line – crab walks
3rd. Tunnel – crawl through

Game – Front and Back
Story Time

Counts	Steps	Arms
Start with Chorus		
1 s/o 8	Standing in 1st	Port de bras—arms low 5th, 1st, high 5th, and to 2nd
1 s/o 8	Standing in 1st	Reverse port de bras
1 – 4	Jump 2nd to 1st	Open to 2nd, close to 1st
5 – 8	Jumps in 1st (2 times)	Arms in 1st
1 – 4	Jump 2nd to 1st	Open to 2nd, close to 1st
5 – 8	Jumps in 1st (2 times)	Arms in 1st
4 s/o 8	Repeat 1st 4 s/o 8	
2 s/o 8	5 tendus from 1st, right, left, right, left, right	Hands on hips
5 – 8 + 1 s/o 8	Bounces, feet together	Hands on tummy
1 s/o 8	Standing in 1st	Port de bras—arms low 5th, 1st, high 5th, and to 2nd
1 s/o 8	Standing in 1st	Reverse port de bras
1 – 4	Jump 2nd to 1st	Open to 2nd, close to 1st
5 – 8	Jumps in 1st (2 times)	Arms in 1st
1 – 4	Jump 2nd to 1st	Open to 2nd, close to 1st
5 – 8	Jump to 2nd, finish	Arms up in a high V

Line up; Share time
Walk into Room

Ballet
Warm-up in center
- Positions in 1st and 2nd
- Demi-pliés in 1st and 2nd
- Tendus front and back
- Kicks front and back

Across Floor
- Ballerina walks on relevé
- Chassés sideways
- Hopscotch with place markers

Center
- Port de bras
- Jumps in 1st, then 1st to 2nd

Monthly Dance – "Never Fully Dressed" from the musical *Annie*
Free Dance – with picture book and CD
Directional Song – "LEFT AND RIGHT MACHINE- The Robot Song"
Game – Front and Back

Tumbling
Stretching
- Head – sideways, shoulder-to-shoulder, up and down, circle
- Arms – hug, arm circles, reaches right and left
- Butterfly

Progressions
- Hops backwards with two feet
- Frog jumps
- Log rolls
- Army drags

Balance Beam
- Walk forward with beanbag on your head

Obstacle Course
1st. Balance Beam – walk forward with beanbag on your head
2nd. Hopscotch – with hula-hoops
3rd. Trampoline – jump 10 times

Game – Parachute Tag
Story Time

Counts	Steps	Arms
Hold till lyrics begin		
1 – 4	Tendu right foot front, close 1st	Hands on hips
5 – 8	Tendu right foot side, close 1st	Hands on hips
1 s/o 8	Repeat tendus	
1 s/o 8	4 chassés to right	Arms out to sides
1 s/o 8	Stand in 1st	Bring fingers across mouth in a smile
1 – 4	Tendu left foot front, close 1st	Hands on hips
5 – 8	Tendu left foot side, close 1st	Hands on hips
1 s/o 8	Repeat tendus	
1 s/o 8	4 chassés to left	Arms out to sides
1 s/o 8	Stand in 1st	Bring fingers across mouth in a smile
1 – 4	Plié in 1st	Hands on hips
5 – 8	Relevé in 1st	Hands on hips
2 s/o 8	Repeat plié and relevé 2 times	
1 s/o 8	Stand in 1st	Touch hands to head, shoulders, then toes
1 s/o 8	Roll body up slowly	Port de bras arms
2 s/o 8	Spin around 2 times	Arms up in high 5th
1 – 4	Tendu right foot front, close 1st	Hands on hips
5 – 8	Tendu right foot side, close 1st	Hands on hips
1 s/o 8	Repeat tendus	
1 s/o 8	4 chassés to right	Arms out to sides
1 s/o 8	Stand in 1st	Bring fingers across mouth in a smile

Line up; Share time
Walk into room

<u>Ballet</u>
Warm-up in center
- Positions in 1st and 2nd
- Demi pliés in 1st and 2nd
- Tendus front and back
- Kicks front and back

Across Floor
- Ballerina walks on relevé
- Chassés sideways
- Turns

Center
- Jumps – in 1st; 1st to 2nd
- ½ turn jumps (jump to face back of room and jump to face front of room)

Monthly Dance –"A Dream is a Wish Your Heart Makes" from Disney's *Cinderella*
Free Dance – with scarves
Directional Song – "I'm Going on a Bear Hunt"
Game – Parachute Tag

<u>Tumbling</u>
Stretching
- Head – sideways, shoulder-to-shoulder, up and down, circle
- Arms – hug, arm circles, reaches right and left
- Straddle on floor – reach right, left, and center

Progressions
- Hops backwards on two feet
- Frog jumps
- Log rolls
- Army drags

Balance Beam
- Walk forward with beanbag balancing on the palm of your hand

Obstacle Course
1st. Balance Beam – walk forward with beanbag balancing on the palm of your hand
2nd. Cones – walk around them on toes
3rd. Tunnel – crawl through forward

Game – "Mother, May I?"
Story Time

Monthly Dance 5 Petite A
"A Dream is a Wish Your Heart Makes" from Disney's **Cinderella**

Counts	Steps	Arms
2 s/o 6	4 slow walks forward	Hands on heart
2 s/o 6	Stand in 1ˢᵗ	Bring arms from right side over head to left, placing head on hands like a pillow
2 s/o 6	4 walks forward	Hands on heart
2 s/o 6	4 slow tendus (right, left, right left)	Hands on heart
2 s/o 6	4 turns to right	Hands on shoulders
2 s/o 6	4 slow tendus (right, left, right left)	Hands on heart
2 s/o 6	4 chassés to left	Arms out to sides
2 s/o 6	4 walks around self in a circle	Hands on hips
1 s/o 6	Sit down on knees	
1 s/o 6	On knees	Port de bras arms through high 5ᵗʰ; place hands on heart

Line up; Share time
Walk into room

Ballet
Warm-up in center
- Positions in 1st and 2nd
- Demi pliés in 1st and 2nd
- Tendus front and back
- Kicks front and back

Across Floor
- Ballerina walks on relevé forward
- Chassés sideways
- Turns

Barre – both hands on the barre
- Plié and relevé in 1st
- Jumps in 1st positions
- Passé

Monthly Dance – "Singin' in the Rain" by Gene Kelly
Free Dance – with maracas
Directional Song – "The Hokey Pokey"
Game – "Mother May I"

Tumbling
Stretching
- Head – sideways, shoulder-to-shoulder, up and down, circle
- Arms – hug, arm circles, reaches right and left
- Straddle on floor – reach right, left, and center

Progressions
- Hop forwards on one foot
- Frog jump
- Pencil rolls
- Seal walks

Balance Beam
- Step passé

Obstacle Coarse
1st. Balance Beam – step passé
2nd. Hopscotch – with stars
3rd. Trampoline – tuck jump

Game – Kangaroo Hop
Story Time

Counts	Steps	Arms
Hold till lyrics begin		
1 – 4	Plié in 1st	Hands on hips
5 – 8	Relevé in 1st	Hands on hips
1 s/o 8	Repeat plié, relevé	
1 – 4	Jump 2nd	Arms open to 2nd
5 – 8	Jump close to 1st	Arms close to 1st
1 s/o 8	Repeat jumps	
1 – 4	Plié in 1st	Hands on hips
5 – 8	Relevé in 1st	Hands on hips
1 s/o 8	Repeat plié, relevé	
1 – 4	Jump 2nd	Arms open to 2nd
5 – 8	Jump close to 1st	Arms close to 1st
1 s/o 8	Repeat jumps	
1 s/o 8	Chassé to right 2 times	Arms out to side
1 – 4	Tendu right to side, passé right	Hands on hips
5 – 8	Close to 1st and hold	
1 s/o 8	Chassé to left 2 times	Arms out to side
1 – 4	Tendu left side passé	Hands on hips
5 – 8	Close to 1st and hold	
2 s/o 8	Walks on relevé forward	Hands on hips
1 – 4	Tendu passé right	Hands on hips
5 – 8	Close to 1st and hold	
1 – 4	Pose down on 1 knee	Arms out to side

Line up; Share time
Walk into room

Ballet
Warm-up in center
- Positions in 1st and 2nd
- Demi pliés in 1st, 2nd, and 3rd
- Tendus front, side, and back
- Kicks front, side, and back

Across Floor
- Ballerina walks on relevé, forward
- Chassés forward
- Turns

Barre – both hands on the barre
- Plié and relevé in 1st
- Tendu side, passé
- Arabesque

Monthly Dance – "Part of your World" from Disney's *The Little Mermaid*
Free Dance – with ribbons
Directional Song – "Head Shoulders Knees and Toes"
Game – Kangaroo Hop

Tumbling
Stretching
- Head – sideways, shoulder-to-shoulder, up and down, circle
- Arms – hug, arm circles, reaches right and left
- Splits on one side

Progressions
- Hop on one foot
- Frog jumps
- Forward rolls

Balance Beam
- Monkey jumps
- Balance in arabesque

Obstacle Coarse
1st. Balance Beam – monkey jump
2nd. Hopscotch – with hula-hoops
3rd. Tunnel – crawl forward

Game – Sticky Popcorn
Story Time

Counts	Steps	Arms
Start on knees with arms in low "V"		
1 s/o 8	Stand up to 1st	Port de bras arms 1st, to high 5th to 2nd
2 s/o 8	Walk forwards	
1 s/o 8	Stand in 1st	Shrug shoulders
1 s/o 8	4 jump in 1st	Hands on hips
1 s/o 8	4 jump 2nd	Hands on hips
1 s/o 8	4 jumps in 1st	Hands on hips
1 s/o 8	Stand in 1st	Shrug shoulders
3 s/o 8	Repeat jumps	Hands on hips
1 s/o 8	Stand in 1st	Shrug shoulders
1 s/o 8	Turn around 2 times	Arms in high 5th
1 s/o 8	2 chassé to right	Arms side
1 s/o 8	Arabesque right, hold	Arms side
1 s/o 8	2 chassé to left	Arms side
1 s/o 8	Arabesque left, hold	Arms side
4 s/o 8	Repeat chassé arabesque hold right and left	
2 s/o 8	Slow walks on relevé forward	
1 s/o 8	Stand in 1st	Reach right hand down to right, left hand down to left
1 s/o 8	Sit down on knees	Port de bras arms 1st, to high 5th to 2nd

Line up; Share time
Walk into room

Ballet
Warm-up in center

- Positions in 1st and 2nd
- Demi-pliés in 1st, 2nd, and 3rd
- Tendus front, side, and back
- Kicks front, side, and back

Across Floor

- Ballerina walks on relevé, forward and sideways
- Chassés forward
- Turns

Center

- Jumps open to 2nd and close to 1st
- Tendu side, passé, tendu side, close to 1st

Barre – both hands on the barre

- Plié and relevé in 1st
- Tendu back, lift to arabesque and hold

Arabesque Monthly Dance – "Rainbow Connection" from The Muppet Movie
Free Dance – with picture book and CD
Directional Song – "London Bridge is Falling Down"
Game – Sticky Popcorn

Tumbling
Stretching

- Head – sideways, shoulder-to-shoulder, up and down, circle
- Arms – hug, arm circles, reaches right and left
- Splits on one side

Progressions

- Step hop, right and left
- Frog jump
- Forward rolls

Balance Beam

- Monkey jumps
- Walk backwards with beanbag on head

Obstacle Coarse

1st. Balance Beam – walk backwards with beanbag on head
2nd. Cones – camel walks around cones
3rd. Trampoline – straddle jump

Game – Monkey Say Monkey Do
Story Time

Counts	Steps	Arms
2 s/o 6	Hold	
1 s/o 6	Plié in 1st	Hands on hips
1 s/o 6	Relevé in 1st	Hands on hips
1 s/o 6	Plié in 1st	Hands on hips
1 s/o 6	Relevé in 1st	Hands on hips
1 s/o 6	2 chassé to right	Arms out to side
1 s/o 6	Tendu right to side, passé, tendu, close 1st	Hands on hips
1 s/o 6	2 chassé to left	Arms out to side
1 s/o 6	Tendu left to side, passé, tendu, close 1st	Hands on hips
4 s/o 6	Repeat chasse, tendu passé combination from above	
1 s/o 6	4 kicks front	Arms out to side
1 s/o 6	4 kicks back	Arms out to side
1 s/o 6	Plié in 1st	Hands on hips
1 s/o 6	Relevé in 1st	Hands on hips
1 s/o 6	Plié in 1st	Hands on hips
1 s/o 6	Relevé in 1st	Hands on hips
1 s/o 6	Stand in 1st	Reach right hand down to right, left hand down to left
1 s/o 6	Stand in 1st	port de bras arms 1st, to high 5th to 2nd

Line up; Share time
Walk into room

Ballet
Warm-up in center
- Positions in 1st and 2nd

Across Floor
- Ballerina walks on relevé, forward and sideways
- Chassés forward
- Turns

Center
- Jumps open to 2nd and close to 1st
- Tendu side, passé, tendu side, close to 1st

Barre – both hands on the barre
- Demi-pliés in 1st, 2nd and 3rd
- Tendus front, side, and back
- Kicks front, side, and back
- Plié and relevé in 1st
- Tendu back, lift to arabesque and hold

Monthly Dance – "Wind Beneath my Wings" by Bette Midler
Free Dance – with scarves
Directional Song – "LEFT AND RIGHT MACHINE- The Robot Song"
Game – Monkey Says, Monkey Do.

Tumbling
Stretching
- Head – sideways, shoulder-to-shoulder, up and down, circle
- Arms – hug, arm circles, reaches right and left
- Splits on one side

Progressions
- Skips (step hop, step hop)
- Frog jumps
- Straddle forward rolls

Balance Beam
- Monkey jump
- Walk backward with beanbag on head

Obstacle Coarse
1st. Balance Beam – walk backward with beanbag on head
2nd. Line – 3 turns
3rd. Tunnel – crawl backward

Game – Red Light Green Light
Story Time

Counts	Steps	Arms
Hold till lyrics begin		
1 s/o 8	Step right forward, left in arabesque, hold	Arms out to side
1 s/o 8	Step left forward, right in arabesque, hold	Arms out to side
2 s/o 8	Tendu right front, side, back, side	Hands on hips
	(4 counts each)	
1 s/o 8	Step right forward, left in arabesque, hold	Arms out to side
1 s/o 8	Step left forward, right in arabesque, hold	Arms out to side
2 s/o 8	Tendu right front, side, back, side	Hands on hips
	(4 counts each)	
1 – 8, 1 – 4	3 turns right	Arms in 1st
5 – 8	Plié in 1st	Arms in 1st
1 – 8, 1 – 4	3 turns left	Arms in 1st
5 – 8	Plié in 1st	Arms in 1st
4 s/o 8	Repeat turns and plié right and left	Arms in 1st
2 s/o 8	Jumps 2nd to 1st 4 times	Arms open, close
1 s/o 8	Step right forward, left in arabesque, hold	Arms out to side
1 s/o 8	Step left forward, right in arabesque, hold	Arms out to side
2 s/o 8	Jumps 2nd to 1st 4 times	Arms open, close
1 s/o 8	Step right forward, left in arabesque, hold	Arms out to side
1 s/o 8	Step left forward, right in arabesque, hold	Arms out to side

Line up; Share time
Walk into room

<u>Ballet</u>
Warm-up in center
- Positions in 1st and 2nd

Across Floor
- Ballerina walks on relevé, forward and sideways
- Chassés forward
- Turns

Center
- Jumps open to 2nd and close to 1st
- Tendu side, passé, tendu side, close to 1st

Barre – Both hands on the barre
- Demi-pliés in 1st, 2nd and 3rd
- Tendus front, side, and back
- Kicks front, side, and back
- Plié and relevé in 1st
- Tendu back, lift to arabesque and hold

Monthly Dance – "Tomorrow" from the musical *Annie*
Free Dance – with ribbons
Directional Song – "I'm Going on a Bear Hunt"
Game – Red Light, Green Light

<u>Tumbling</u>
Stretching
- Head – sideways, shoulder-to-shoulder, up and down, circle
- Arms – hug, arm circles, reaches right and left
- Splits on one side

Progressions
- Skips
- Frog jump
- Straddle forward rolls

Balance Beam
- Monkey jump
- Step passé

Obstacle Coarse
1st. Balance Beam – step passé
2nd. Hopscotch – with hula-hoops
3rd. Trampoline – straddle jump

Game – Twister Two
Story Time

Counts	Steps	Arms
Hold till lyrics begin		
1 – 4	2 chassé right	Arms out to side
5 – 8	Arabesque left, close 1st	Arms out to side
1 – 4	Tendu right to side, passé,	Hands on hips
5 – 8	Tendu, close first	Hands on hips
2 s/o 8	Repeat to left	
2 s/o 8	Walks forward on relevé	Arms port de bra
1 - 4	turn around 1 time	Arms in high 5th
1 – 4	2 chassé right	Arms out to side
5 – 8	Arabesque left, close 1st	Arms out to side
1 – 4	Tendu right to side, passé,	Hands on hips
5 – 8	Tendu, close first	Hands on hips
1 – 4	2 turns to left	Arms in 1st
5 – 8	Stand in 1st	Hands on heart and reach out to audience
1 – 4	Tendu right to side, passé,	Hands on hips
5 – 8	Tendu close first	Hands on hips

Chapter Five
Petite B Syllabus

- Students wait at the door for the teacher's instruction to enter
- Understands finding their place-makers (colors and/or shapes) as instructed
- Walks "like a dancer" when ever changing locations; does not run
- Students are able to complete all items listed in the Petite A syllabus

Ballet

Center
- Student stands in line with stomach to mirror

Barre
- Student keeps one hand on the barre and is spaced correctly, leaving enough space between themselves and the next student

Across Floor
- Student stays in place; sits with legs crossed and back to wall
- Student understands taking turns

Body Positions with arms 1st, 2nd, and 3rd
- Feet turned out
- Thumbs in
- Arms round in each position

Plié in 1st, 2nd, and 3rd position
- Heels stay on the ground in demi plié
- Knees push out to side making a diamond shape

Tendu in 1st position
- Front, side, and back
- Sliding foot on the ground leaving toe on the ground
- Foot completely extended in tendu

Rond de jambe
- Front, side, and back
- Leg fully extended
- Foot slides though 1st position, equal turn out in 1st
- *Knee facing correct location as leg rotates around*

Kicks

- Front, side, and back
- Kicks as high as he/she can
- Correct direction placement
- Knees straight and/or toes pointed

Chassé side
- Arms in 2nd
- Feet meet in 1st in the air and do not cross
- Plié when landing and taking off
- Feet remain in 1st with toes pointed to either side (turned out)

Chassé front
- Arms in 2nd position
- Feet meeting in 5th position in the air (does not alternate legs)
- Plié when landing and taking off
- Stomach faces direction of movement
- Arms hold still in 2nd

Bourrées in 3rd/5th position
- Sideways and forward
- Stomach to the mirror
- Knees stay straight
- Stay on relieve the whole time
- Arms stay round with thumbs in
- Turned out

Step, passé, close 1st – hands on hips feet in first, slide foot to tendu side, step changing weight, pull other foot to passé, slide toe down leg to 1st position
- Passé is turned out
- Stomach stay facing mirror
- Foot slides to tendu
- Only toe touches at knee
- *Foot is not sickled*

Pas de chat – passé, jump switching weight, passé, close 1st position
- Knees pointed to correct sides (turned out)
- Jump one foot to one foot

Step arabesque – step to arabesque close to 1st
- Stomach facing direction of movement
- Arms in "L"
- Upper body stays up not bent over

Turns – chaînés

- Turning the correct direction
- On toes the hold time
- A concept of spotting

Leaps
- Toes pointed
- Plié at start and end of jump
- Arms stay in 2nd position

Balancé
- Stomach facing mirror whole time
- Changing weight side to side
- Changing from the relieve to flat foot

Sauté – jumps in 1st
- Jumping together as a class and with music or counts
- Plié in 1st at start and end
- Landing in 1st
- Toes pointed and leg straight in the air

Changement in 3rd/5th
- Pliés at start and end of jump
- Switches feet in the air
- *Legs straight and toes pointed in air*

Echappé sauté – jump open to 2nd, close to 1st
- Arms opening and closing with legs
- Pliés in 1st and 2nd
- Jumping together as a class and with music or counts
- Toes pointed and leg straight in the air

Tumbling

- Student sits with legs crossed and back to wall
- Student understands taking turns
- Walks to and from mat; does not, crawl, run, hop, etc.
- Returns to correct spot in line

Frog Jumps
- Starting with hands and feet ground
- Jumping high with arms up and body straight
- *Legs straight and together in the air*
- Landing with hands and feet ground

Jelly/*Pencil* rolls
- Lay across mat on back
- Rolls straight down mat
- Jelly roll arms are by side
- *Pencil rolls arms above head, hands together, elbows straight*
- *Legs straight, toes pointed*

Army drags
- Lay on stomach
- Uses arms and legs to crawl across the mat
- Does not go up on knees

Seal walks
- Stomach on the ground
- Lifts chest up supported by your arms
- Uses arms to walk down the mat

Monkey jumps
- Place both hand on the beam (or a raised mat)
- Jumps feet from one side of beam to the other
- Supports movement with straight arms
- Lands on feet

Camel walks
- Walks on hands and feet
- Keeps knees and elbows straight when walking

Crab/*Table* walks
- Walks on hands and feet with stomach towards the ceiling
- Travels full length of mat
- Crab walk bottom does not touch the ground
- Walks forwards and backwards
- Table walk *stomach pushed up to ceiling creating a table*

Hops on one foot, forward/*backwards*
- *Keeps foot up for full length of mat*
- *Can do with either right or left foot up, not just on one side*

Forward rolls
- Start in a squatting position with head down (chin on chest)
- Rolls straight, keeps head tucked
- *Rolls back onto feet in squatting position without pushing with hands*

Straddle rolls
- Sit in a straddle position
- Tuck head in and do a forward roll leaving legs in the straddle position
- End in a straddle position

Balance Beam
- Walks forward and backwards
- Keeps head up and arms straight out to sides
- Balances in passé (knee faces side); *without assistance*
- Balances in arabesque (leg straight and toes pointed; keeps chest up); *without assistance*

Obstacle Coarse
- Understand four different skills in a row
- Can move from one item to then next in correct order
- Correctly uses each piece of equipment
- *Can reverse the order and/ or perform all tricks backwards*

Tap

Toe tap warm-ups
- Able to balance on one foot
- Correct direction placement
- Student stands in line with stomach to mirror when doing center work
- Correct sound and correct use of foot
- Whole leg moves

Across the floor
- Student sits criss-cross with back to wall
- Keeps feet quite when waiting for their turn
- Students understands taking turns

Center
- Student stands in line with stomach to mirror when doing center work

Walking on tip toes
- Balances on toes the full length of the room
- Hands on hips
- Keeps taps sounds quite

Marches
- Step with whole foot

Heel toe walks
- Hands on hips
- Has correct order
- Equal sounds both heel and toe

Toe heel walks
- Hands on hips
- Has correct order
- Drops heel, not stomps foot
- Equal sounds from both toes and heels

Brush step (Flap)
- Two sounds
- Movement starts from back
- Brushes with toe only

Shuffle
- Two sounds
- Movement starts from back
- Brushes with toe only

Shuffle step
- Three sounds
- Movement starts from back
- Brushes with toe only
- Step is quieter than shuffle

Shuffle hop step
- Four sounds
- Movement starts from back
- Hops on one foot
- Brushes with toe only
- Step is quieter than shuffle

Cramp Rolls
- Four sounds
- Steps on toes
- Drops heels

Chapter Six
Lesson Plans and Monthly Dance for Petite B

Line up; Share time
Walk into room

Ballet
Warm – up in center
- Demi plié in 1st, 2nd, and 3rd with port de bras
- Tendu in 1st front, side, and back
- Kicks front and back

Across Floor
- Bourrée in 1st
- Chassé sideways
- Chaînés turns

Center
- Jumps in 1st, 1st to 2nd

Monthly Dance – "Wind Beneath My Wings" by Bette Midler

Tumbling
Stretching
- Head – sideways, shoulder-to-shoulder, up and down, circle
- Arms – hug, arm circles, reaches right and left
- Touch toes

Progressions
- Hops forward and backwards with two feet
- Pencil rolls
- Monkey jumps

Obstacle Coarse
1st. Balance Beam – monkey jump
2nd. Hopscotch – with hula-hoops
3rd. Tunnel – crawl forward
4th. Trampoline – 10 jumps

Tap
Warm – up
- Toe taps front
- Heel dig front
- Roll ankles

Across Floor
- Walk quite on toes
- Loud marches

Center
- Shuffles

Game – Parachute Tag
Story Time

"Wind Beneath my Wings" by Bette Midler

Counts	Steps	Arms
Hold till lyrics begin		
1 s/o 8	Step right forward, left in arabesque, hold	Arms out to side
1 s/o 8	Step left forward, right in arabesque, hold	Arms out to side
2 s/o 8	Tendu right front, side, back, side	Hands on hips
	(4 counts each)	
1 s/o 8	Step right forward, left in arabesque, hold	Arms out to side
1 s/o 8	Step left forward, right in arabesque, hold	Arms out to side
2 s/o 8	Tendu right front, side, back, side	Hands on hips
	(4 counts each)	
1 – 8, 1 – 4	3 turns right	Arms in 1st
5 – 8	Plié in 1st	Arms in 1st
1 – 8, 1 – 4	3 turns left	Arms in 1st
5 – 8	Plié in 1st	Arms in 1st
4 s/o 8	Repeat turns and plié right and left	Arms in 1st
2 s/o 8	Jumps 2nd to 1st 4 times	Arms open, close
1 s/o 8	Step right forward, left in arabesque, hold	Arms out to side
1 s/o 8	Step left forward, right in arabesque, hold	Arms out to side
2 s/o 8	Jumps 2nd to 1st 4 times	Arms open, close
1 s/o 8	Step right forward, left in arabesque, hold	Arms out to side
1 s/o 8	Step left forward, right in arabesque, hold	Arms out to side

Line up; Share time
Walk into room

Ballet
Warm – up in Center
- Demi plié in 1st, 2nd, and 3rd with port de bras
- Tendu in 1st front, side, and back
- Kicks front and back

Across Floor
- Bourees in 1st
- Chassé sideways
- Chaînés turns

Center
- Jumps in 1st, 1st to 2nd
- Tendu passé

Free Dance – with maracas

Tumbling
Stretching
- Head, arms, and touch toes

Progressions
- Frog jumps
- Pencil rolls
- Walking backwards

Obstacle Coarse
1st. Balance Beam – walk backwards
2nd. Cones – bourrées
3rd. Tunnel – crawl forward
4th. Trampoline – jumps

Tap
Warm – up
- Toe taps front
- Heel digs front
- Roll ankles

Across Floor
- Walk quite on toes forwards and backwards
- Loud marches
- Heel toe walks

Center
- Shuffles

Monthly Dance – "At the Hop" by Danny and the Juniors
Story Time

Counts	Steps	Arms
Hold		Hands on knees
4 s/o 8	Bounces	Hands on knees
1 s/o 8	Jump, shake hips	Hands on hips
1 s/o 8	Toe taps to front with right foot	Hands on hips
1 s/o 8	Stomp together, shake hips	Hands on hips
1 s/o 8	Toe taps to with left foot	Hands on hips
1 s/o 8	Stomp together, shake hips	Hands on hips
1 s/o 8	Toe taps to front with right foot	Hands on hips
1 s/o 8	Stomp together, shake hips	Hands on hips
4 s/o 8	16 toe heel walks forward	Hands on hips
	(2 counts toe, 2 counts heel)	
2 s/o 8	Shuffles right foot	Hands on hips
1 s/o 8	Toe taps to front with left foot	Hands on hips
1 s/o 8	Stomp together, shake hips	Hands on hips
1 s/o 8	Toe taps to with right foot	Hands on hips
1 s/o 8	Stomp together, shake hips	Hands on hips
1 s/o 8	Toe taps to front with left foot	Hands on hips
1 s/o 8	Stomp together, shake hips	Hands on hips
4 s/o 8	16 toe heel walks forward	Hands on hips
	(2 counts toe, 2 counts heel)	
2 s/o 8	Shuffles left foot	Hands on hips
1 – 4	Jump	Arms up

Line up; Share time
Walk into room

Ballet
Warm – up in center
- Demi plié in 1st, 2nd, and 3rd with port de bras
- Tendu in 1st front, side, and back
- Kicks front, side, and back

Across Floor
- Bourrée in 1st
- Turns
- Hopscotch

Center
- Tendu, passé
- Arabesque

Monthly Dance – "Tomorrow" from the musical *Annie*

Tumbling
Stretching
- Head, arms, and butterflies stretch

Progressions
- Camel walks
- Forward rolls

Balance Beam
- Step passé

Obstacle Coarse
1st. Balance Beam – step passé
2nd. Line – camel walks
3rd. Tunnel – crawl backwards
4th. Trampoline – tuck jump

Tap
Warm – up
- Toe taps front and side
- Heel dig front and side
- Roll ankles

Across Floor
- Walk quite on toes forwards and backwards
- Heel toe walks

Center
- Shuffle step

Game – "If Your Happy and You Know It" with the parachute
Story Time

Counts	Steps	Arms
Hold till lyrics begin		
1 – 4	2 chassé right	Arms out to side
5 – 8	Arabesque left, close 1st	Arms out to side
1 – 4	Tendu right to side, passé,	Hands on hips
5 – 8	Tendu, close first	Hands on hips
2 s/o 8	Repeat to left	
2 s/o 8	Walks forward on relevé	Arms port de bra
1 - 4	turn around 1 time	Arms in high 5th
1 – 4	2 chassé right	Arms out to side
5 – 8	Arabesque left, close 1st	Arms out to side
1 – 4	Tendu right to side, passé,	Hands on hips
5 – 8	Tendu, close first	Hands on hips
1 – 4	2 turns to left	Arms in 1st
5 – 8	Stand in 1st	Hands on heart and reach out to audience
1 – 4	Tendu right to side, passé,	Hands on hips
5 – 8	Tendu close first	Hands on hips

Line up; Share time
Walk into room

Ballet
Warm – up at the barre
- Demi plié in 1st, 2nd, and 3rd with port de bras
- Tendu in 1st front, side, and back
- Kicks front, side, and back

Across Floor
- Bourrée in 1st
- Chaînés turns
- Skips

Center
- Tendu, passé
- 1st, tendu, arabesque

Free Dance – with picture book and CD

Tumbling
Stretching
- Head, arms, and straddle stretch

Progressions
- Hops backward on two feet
- Straddle rolls

Balance Beam
- Walk forward with beanbag on head

Obstacle Coarse
1st. Balance Beam – walk forward with beanbag on head
2nd. Hopscotch – with place markers
3rd. Tunnel – crawl forward
4th. Trampoline – straddle jump

Tap
Warm – up
- Toe taps front and side
- Heel dig front and side
- Roll ankles

Across Floor
- Walk quite on toes forwards and backwards
- Heel toe walks
- Toe heel walks

Center
- Shuffles and shuffle step

Monthly Dance – "Locomotion" by Grand Funk Railroad
Story Time

Counts	Steps	Arms
1 s/o 8	Hold	Hands on hips
1 s/o 8	Toe heel walks 4 times	Hands on hips
1 – 4	Shuffle step	Hands on hips
5 – 8	Shuffle step	Hands on hips
2 s/o 8	Repeat toe heel walks and shuffle steps	Hands on hips
2 s/o 8	Repeat toe heel walks and shuffle steps	Hands on hips
1 – 6	1 stomp forward	Use hands to say come here
7 & 8		Point to self
1 s/o 8	Swing hips	
1 – 4	Jump forward	Clap
5 – 8	Jump back	Clap
1 s/o 8	Shuffle step 2 times	Hands on Hips
(Face right and follow leader around room)		
1 s/o 8	Toe heel walks 4 times	Hands on hips
1 – 4	Shuffle step	Hands on hips
5 – 8	Shuffle step	Hands on hips
2 s/o 8	Repeat toe heel walks and shuffle steps	Hands on hips
2 s/o 8	Repeat toe heel walks and shuffle steps	Hands on hips
1 – 6	1 stomp forward	Use hands to say come here
7 & 8		Point to self

Line up; Share time
Walk into room

Ballet
Warm – up at the barre
- Demi plié in 1st, 2nd, and 3rd with port de bras
- Tendu from 1st front, side, and back
- Rond de jambe front
- Kicks front and back

Across Floor
- Chaînés turns
- Step passé

Center
- Balancé
- Tendu to side, passé, tendu side, close to 1st
- Tendu back, arabesque, tendu back, close 1st

Monthly Dance – "When You Wish Upon a Star" from Disney's *Pinocchio*

Tumbling
Stretching
- Head, arms, and straddle

Progressions
- Crab walks
- Straddle rolls

Balance Beam
- Monkey jumps

Obstacle Coarse
1st. Balance Beam – monkey jump
2nd. Cones – bourrées
3rd. Tunnel – crawl forward
4th. Trampoline – 10 jumps

Tap
Warm – up
- Toe taps front, side, and back
- Heel dig front and side
- Roll ankles

Across Floor
- Heel toe walks
- Toe heel walks

Center
- Shuffles and shuffle step

Game – Parachute with beanbags
Story Time

"When You Wish Upon a Star" from Disney's **Pinocchio**

Counts	Steps	Arms
Hold till lyrics begin		
2 s/o 8	Step passé 4 times to right	Arms 2nd
2 s/o 8	Step passé 4 times to left	Arms 2nd
1 s/o 8	Bourrées forward	Arms in high 5th
1 s/o 8	Balancé right and left	Arms 2nd
1 s/o 8	Bourrées backward	Arms in high 5th
1 s/o 8	Balancé right and left	Arms in 2nd
1 s/o 8	Chaînés turns right 2 times	Arms in 1st
1 s/o 8	Tendu side, passé, arabesque, passé, close 1st with right foot	Arms in 2nd
1 s/o 8	Chaînés turns left 2 times	Arms in 1st
1 s/o 8	Tendu side, passé, arabesque, passé, close 1st with left foot	Arms in 2nd
1 – 4	Step to right and curtsey	Arms in demi 2nd

Line up; Share time
Walk into room

Ballet
Warm – up at the barre
- Demi plié in 1st, 2nd, and 3rd with port de bras
- Tendu from 1st front, side, and back
- Rond de jambe front
- Kicks front, side, and back

Across Floor
- Chaînés turns
- Step arabesque

Center
- Jumps 1st to 2nd
- Balancé

Free Dance – with maracas

Tumbling
Stretching
- Head, arms, and touch toes

Progressions
- Hops forward on one foot
- Forward straddle rolls
- Cartwheel

Obstacle Coarse
1st. Mat – cartwheel
2nd. Hopscotch – with place markers
3rd. Tunnel – crawl backward
4th. Trampoline – tuck jumps

Tap
Warm – up
- Toe taps front, side, and back
- Heel dig front and back
- Roll ankles

Across Floor
- Heel toe walks
- Toe heel walks

Center
- Shuffle step
- Shuffle hop step
- Cramp rolls

Monthly Dance – "Rockin' Robin" by Bobby Day
Story Time

Counts	Steps	Arms
4 s/o 8	Bounces	Hands on knees
2 s/o 8	Shuffle steps 4 times	Hands on hips
2 s/o 8	Heel dig step 4 times	Hands on hips
2 s/o 8	Shuffle hop step 2 times	Hands on hips
2 s/o 8	Toe back step 4 times	Hands on hips
2 s/o 8	4 toe heel walk forward	Hands on hips
2 s/o 8	Shuffle step 4 times	Hands on hips
2 s/o 8	4 heel toe walks forward	Hands on hips
2 s/o 8	Shuffle step 4 times	Hands on hips
1 – 4	Jump forward	Clap
5 – 8	Jump back	Clap
1 s/o 8	Twist	
1 – 4	Jump forward	Clap
5 – 8	Jump back	Clap
1 s/o 8	Twist	
1 – 4	Jump forward	Clap
5 – 8	Jump back	Clap
1 s/o 8	Twist	
2 s/o 8	Bounces	Hands on knees
1 s/o 8	Shuffle hop step	Hands on hips
1 – 4	Jump forward clap	Hands on hips
5 – 8	Jump back clap	Hands on hips
2 s/o 8	Shuffle steps 4 times	Hands on hips
2 s/o 8	Heel dig step 4 times	Hands on hips

Line up; Share time
Walk into Room

Ballet
Warm – up at the barre
- Demi plié in 1st, 2nd, and 3rd with port de bras
- Tendu from 1st front, side, and back
- Rond de jambe front
- Kicks front and back

Across Floor
- Chaînés turns
- Step passé
- Step arabesque, hop

Center
- Jumps 1st to 2nd
- Balancé

Monthly Dance – "When will my Life Begin" from Disney's *Tangled*

Tumbling
Stretching
- Head, arms, and splits right and left

Progressions
- Forward straddle rolls
- Cartwheel

Obstacle Coarse
1st. Mat – forward roll to standing
2nd. Hopscotch – hula-hoops
3rd. Tunnel – crawl forward
4th. Trampoline – straddle jump

Tap
Warm – up
- Toe taps front, side, and back
- Heel dig front and side
- Roll ankles

Across Floor
- Heel toe walks
- Toe heel walks

Center
- Shuffle step & shuffle hop step
- Heel dig side, toe back, heel dig side, step together
- Cramp roll

Game – Parachute Tag
Story Time

Monthly Dance 7 Petite B
"When will my Life Begin" from Disney's **Tangled**

Counts	Steps	Arms
Hold till lyrics begin		
1 – 4	Plié in 1st	Hands on hips
5 – 8	Relevé in 1st	Hands on hips
2 s/o 8	Repeat plié relevé 2 times	Hands on hips
1 s/o 8	Step arabesque hop right, left, right, left	Arms 2nd
1 s/o 8	Round de jambe right and left	Arms 2nd
2 s/o 8	Repeat step arabesque hops and round de jambe	
1 – 6	Chaînés turns right 3	Arms 1st
7 & 8	Curtsey	Arms demi 2nd
1 s/o 8	Repeat chaînés turns and curtsey to left	
1 s/o 8	Jump 2nd to 1st 2 times	Arms 2nd to 1st
1 s/o 8	Balancé right and left	Arms 2nd
2 s/o 8	Bourrées back	Arms in high 5th
4 s/o 8	Step arabesque hops and round de jambe	
	2 times	Arms in 2nd
2 s/o 8	Chaînés turns and curtsey right and left	
1 s/o 8	Stand in 1st	Arms port de bra

Line up; Share time
Walk into room

Ballet
Warm – up at the barre
- Demi plié in 1st, 2nd, and 3rd with port de bras and balance in relevé
- Tendu from 1st front, side, and back
- Rond de jambe front
- Kicks front and back

Across Floor
- Chaînés turns
- Step passé on relevé
- Step arabesque hop

Center
- Changment
- Pas de chat

Free Dance – with picture book and CD

Tumbling
Stretching
- Head, arms, and splits right and left

Progressions
- Backward roll
- Cartwheel

Balance Beam
- Bridge

Obstacle Coarse
1st. Mat – forward roll
2nd. Tunnel – crawl backwards
3rd. Cones – camel walks
4th. Trampoline – 10 jumps

Tap
Warm – up
- Toe taps front, side, and back
- Heel dig front, side, and back
- Roll ankles

Across Floor
- Flaps and flap heel

Center
- Shuffle step & shuffle hop step
- Heel dig side, toe back, heel dig side, step together
- Cramp roll

Monthly Dance – "I'm So Excited" by The Pointer Sisters
Story Time

Counts	Steps	Arms
4 s/o 8	Hold	Hands on hips
2 s/o 8	Cramp roll 2 times	Hands on hips
2 s/o 8	Flaps right, left, right and left	Hands on hips
2 s/o 8	Cramp roll 2 times	Hands on hips
2 s/o 8	Flaps right, left, right and left	Hands on hips
2 s/o 8	Step touch right, left, right, left	Hands on hips
1 s/o 8	Shuffle step right and left	Hands on hips
1 s/o 8	Shuffle hop step right and left	Hands on hips
2 s/o 8	Step touch right, left, right, left	Hands on hips
1 s/o 8	Shuffle step right and left	Hands on hips
1 s/o 8	Shuffle hop step right and left	Hands on hips
4 s/o 8	4 cramp rolls facing front, right side, back, left side	Hands on hips
2 s/o 8	2 cramps rolls front	Hands on hips
1 – 4	Jump up	Arms reaching up
12 counts	Bounces	Hands on hips
2 s/o 8	Step touch right, left, right and left	Hands on hips
1 – 4	Jump up	Arms reaching up
12 counts	Bounces	Hands on hips
2 s/o 8	Step touch right, left, right and left	Hands on hips

Line up; Share time
Walk into room

Ballet
Warm – up at the barre
- Demi plié in 1st, 2nd, and 3rd with port de bras and balance in relevé
- Tendu from 1st front, side, and back
- Rond de jambe front and back
- Kicks front, side, and back

Across Floor
- Chaînés turns
- Step passé on relevé

Center
- Pas de chat
- Changement

Monthly Dance – "Lets Go Fly a Kite" from Disney's *Mary Poppins*

Tumbling
Stretching
- Head, arms, and splits right and left

Progressions
- Forward straddle rolls to standing
- Cartwheel

Balance Beam
- Bridge up over beam

Obstacle Coarse
1st. Mat – forward straddle rolls to standing
2nd. Line – 3 chaînés turns
3rd. Tunnel – crawl forward
4th. Trampoline – straddle jump

Tap
Warm – up
- Toe taps – front, side, and back
- Heel digs – front and side
- Roll ankles

Across Floor
- Flaps and flap heel

Center
- Shuffle touch
- Shuffle step and shuffle hop step
- Heel dig side, toe back, heel dig side, step together

Game – "If You're Happy and You Know It" with the parachute
Story Time

Counts	Steps	Arms
2 s/o 6	Tendu, close 1st – right foot front, side,	
	back, side	Arms 2nd
2 s/o 86	Tendu, close 1st – left foot front, side,	
	back, side	Arms 2nd
1 s/o 6	Relevé in 1st and hold	Arms in high 5th
3 s/o 8	Pas de chat 3 times to right	
	(passé right, jump passé left, close 1st)	Hands on hips
1 s/o 6	Walks around self	Arms demi 2nd
3 s/o 6	Pas de chat 3 times to left	Hands on hips
1 s/o 6	Walks around self	Arms demi 2nd
3 s/o 6	Relevé in 1st and hold	Arms in high 5th
3 s/o 6	Pas de chat 3 times to right	Hands on hips
1 s/o 6	Walks around self	Arms demi 2nd
3 s/o 6	Pas de chat 3 times to left	Hands on hips
1 s/o 6	Walks around self	Arms demi 2nd
	Relevé in 1st	Arms in high 5th

Line up; Share time
Walk into room

Ballet
Warm – up at the barre
- Demi plié in 1st, 2nd, and 3rd with port de bras and balance in relevé
- Tendu from 1st front, side, and back
- Rond de jambe front and back
- Kicks front and back

Across Floor
- Turns
- Pas de chat

Free Dance – with ribbons

Tumbling
Stretching
- Head, arms, and splits right and left

Progressions
- Forward rolls to standing
- Backward rolls to standing

Balance Beam
- Step passé

Obstacle Coarse
1st. Mat – cartwheel
2nd. Hopscotch – hula-hoops
3rd. Tunnel – crawl backwards
4th. Trampoline – straddle Jump

Tap
Warm – up
- Toe taps front, side, and back
- Heel digs front and side
- Roll ankles

Across Floor
- Toe heel walks
- Flaps and flap heel

Center
- Shuffle touch, shuffle step & shuffle hop step
- Heel dig side, toe back, heel dig side, step together

Monthly Dance – "Stupid Cupid" by Connie Francis
Story Time

Counts	Steps	Arms
Hold till lyrics begin		
4 s/o 8	Heel dig front, toe to back, heel dig front,	
	step together (2 counts each) – right, left,	
	right, left	Hands on hips
1 s/o 8	Feet together move heels right, left, right, left	Hands on heart
1 – 4	Jump feet a part	Arms out to side
5 – 8	Hold	Hands point to self
		on word "me"
1 – 4	Toe heel right and left	Hands on hips
5 – 8	Shuffle hop step right	Hands on hips
1 – 4	Toe heel left and right	Hands on hips
5 – 8	Shuffle hop step left	Hands on hips
1 s/o 8	Repeat toe heels, shuffle hop step right and left	
1 s/o 8	Feet together move heels right, left, right, left	Hands on heart
1 – 4	Jump feet a part	Arms out to side
5 – 8	Hold	Hands point to self
		word "me"
3 s/o 8	Step right foot to side,	
	shuffle hop step left foot – 3 times	hands out to side
1 s/o 8	Feet together move heels right, left, right, left	Hands on heart
4 s/o 8	Heel side, toe back, heel side, step together	Hands on hips
1 s/o 8	Feet together move heels right, left, right, left	Hands on heart
1 – 4	Jump feet a part	Arms out to side
5 – 8	Hold	Hands point to self
		on word "me"

Chapter Seven
Petite C Syllabus

- Students wait at the door for the teacher's instruction to enter
- Understands finding their place-makers (colors and/or shapes) as instructed
- Walks "Like a dancer" when ever changing locations; does not run
- Students are able to complete all items listed in the Petite A and B syllabi

Ballet

Plié – 1st, 2nd, and 3rd position in demi and grande
- Heels stay on the ground in demi pile
- Knees push out to side making a diamond shape

Tendu – front, side, and back in 1st position with hands on hips
- Sliding foot on the ground leaving toe on the ground
- Foot completely extended in tendu

Rond de jambe – forwards and backwards
- Leg fully extended
- Foot slides though 1st position, equal turn out in 1st
- Knee facing correct location as leg rotates around

Kicks – front, side, and back
- Kicks as high as he/she can
- Correct direction placement
- Knees straight and/or toes pointed
- Does not move from the line

Chaînés turns
- Turning the correct direction
- On toes the hold time
- Spotting
- Arms stay in 1st
- Turning in 1st

Pique turns
- Turning correct direction
- Toe only touches at knee, knee turned out, foot not sickled
- On relevé keeping the knee straight
- Spots

Balancé
- Stomach facing mirror whole time
- Changing sides
- Changing from the relieve to flat foot

Changement in 3rd/5th
- Pliés at start and end of jump
- Switches feet in the air
- Legs straight and toes pointed in air

Pas de bourrée
- Back, side, front movement
- Uses full relevé
- Ends in demi plié

Assemblé
- Brushes foot to side
- Jumps from one foot
- Feet hit in air
- Lands on two feet in demi plié

Sauté arabesque
- Jumps and lands on one foot in demi plié
- Holds arabesque while jumping

Tap

Flap
- 2 sounds
- Movement starts from back
- Brushes with toe only

Flap heel
- 3 sounds
- Movement starts from back
- Brushes with toe only
- Drops heel
- Changes weight

Flap ball change
- 4 sounds
- Movement starts from the back
- Brushes with toe only
- Correct syncopation for ball change

Shuffle
- 2 sounds
- Movement starts from back
- Brushes with toe only

Shuffle touch
- Touches toe to foot without changing weight

Shuffle step
- 3 sounds
- Movement starts from back
- Brushes with toe only
- Step is quieter than shuffle

Shuffle hop step
- 3 sounds
- Movement starts from back
- Hops on one foot
- Brushes with toe only
- Step is quieter than shuffle

Shuffle ball change
- 4 sounds
- Movement starts from back
- Brushes with toe only
- Correct syncopation for ball change

Buffalo
- Changes weight from one foot to the other
- Able to balance holding one foot in the air
- Shuffle using only toe sounds, no heels

Maxie ford
- Changes weight from one foot to the other
- Able to balance holding one foot in the air
- Shuffle using only toe sounds, no heels
- *Turns*

Chapter Eight

Lesson Plans and Monthly Dance for Petite C

Line up; Share time
Walk into room

Ballet
Warm – up at the barre
- Demi plié in 1st, 2nd, and 3rd
- Tendu from 1st to front, side, and back
- Rond de jambe front
- Kicks front and side

Stretching
- Butterflies
- Straddle
- Splits right and left

Across Floor
- Bourrées
- Chaînés turns
- Step passé

Center
- Tendu, passé, arabesque, passé, close to 1st
- Balancé
- Echappé

Free Dance – with picture book and CD

Tap
Warm – up
- Toe taps front, side, and back
- Heel digs front and side
- Heel drops
- Roll ankles

Across Floor
- Toe heel walks
- Flaps
- Flap heel

Center
- Shuffle step
- Shuffle hop step
- Step side, toe to the back, clap

Monthly Dance – "I'm So Excited" by The Pointer Sisters
Story Time

Counts	Steps	Arms
4 s/o 8	Hold	Hands on hips
2 s/o 8	Cramp roll 2 times	Hands on hips
2 s/o 8	Flaps right, left, right and left	Hands on hips
2 s/o 8	Cramp roll 2 times	Hands on hips
2 s/o 8	Flaps right, left, right and left	Hands on hips
2 s/o 8	Step touch right, left, right, left	Hands on hips
1 s/o 8	Shuffle step right and left	Hands on hips
1 s/o 8	Shuffle hop step right and left	Hands on hips
2 s/o 8	Step touch right, left, right, left	Hands on hips
1 s/o 8	Shuffle step right and left	Hands on hips
1 s/o 8	Shuffle hop step right and left	Hands on hips
4 s/o 8	4 cramp rolls facing front, right side,	
	back, left side	Hands on hips
2 s/o 8	2 cramps rolls front	Hands on hips
1 – 4	Jump up	Arms reaching up
12 counts	Bounces	Hands on hips
2 s/o 8	Step touch right, left, right and left	Hands on hips
1 – 4	Jump up	Arms reaching up
12 counts	Bounces	Hands on hips
2 s/o 8	Step touch right, left, right and left	Hands on hips

Line up; Share time
Walk into room

Ballet
Warm – up at the barre
- Demi plié in 1st, 2nd, and 3rd
- Grande plié in 1st
- Tendu from 1st to front, side, and back
- Rond de jambe front
- Kicks front and side

Stretching
- Butterflies
- Straddle
- Splits right and left

Across Floor
- Bourrée
- Chaîné turns
- Step passé

Center
- Tendu, passé, arabesque, passé, close to 1st
- Échappé

Monthly Dance – "Lets Go Fly a Kite" from Disney's *Mary Poppins*

Tap
Warm – up
- Toe taps front, side, and back
- Heel digs front and side
- Heel drops
- Roll ankles

Across Floor
- Toe heel walks
- Flap
- Flap heel
- Flap ball change

Center
- Shuffle step
- Shuffle hop step
- Step, toe to the back, clap

Game – Parachute Tag
Story Time

Counts	Steps	Arms
2 s/o 6	Tendu, close 1st – right foot front, side,	
	back, side	Arms 2nd
2 s/o 86	Tendu, close 1st – left foot front, side,	
	back, side	Arms 2nd
1 s/o 6	Relevé in 1st and hold	Arms in high 5th
3 s/o 8	Pas de chat 3 times to right	
	(passé right, jump passé left, close 1st)	Hands on hips
1 s/o 6	Walks around self	Arms demi 2nd
3 s/o 6	Pas de chat 3 times to left	Hands on hips
1 s/o 6	Walks around self	Arms demi 2nd
3 s/o 6	Relevé in 1st and hold	Arms in high 5th
3 s/o 6	Pas de chat 3 times to right	Hands on hips
1 s/o 6	Walks around self	Arms demi 2nd
3 s/o 6	Pas de chat 3 times to left	Hands on hips
1 s/o 6	Walks around self	Arms demi 2nd
	Relevé in 1st	Arms in high 5th

Line up; Share time
Walk into room

Ballet
Warm – up at the barre
- Demi plié in 1st, 2nd, and 3rd
- Grande plié in 1st
- Tendu from 1st to front, side, and back
- Rond de jambe front
- Kicks front and side

Stretching
- Straddle
- Splits right, center, and left

Across Floor
- Chaîné turns
- Step piqué passé on relevé

Center
- Balancé
- Échappé
- Pas de chat
- Changement

Free Dance – with scarves

Tap
Warm – up
- Toe taps front, side, and back
- Heel digs front and side
- Heel drops
- Roll ankles

Across Floor
- Flap
- Flap heel
- Flap ball change

Center
- Shuffle step
- Shuffle hop step
- Heel dig, toe to the back, heel dig, step

Monthly Dance – "Stupid Cupid" by Connie Francis
Story Time

Counts	Steps	Arms
Hold till lyrics begin		
4 s/o 8	Heel dig front, toe to back, heel dig front,	
	step together (2 counts each) – right, left,	
	right, left	Hands on hips
1 s/o 8	Feet together move heels right, left, right, left	Hands on heart
1 – 4	Jump feet a part	Arms out to side
5 – 8	Hold	Hands point to self
		on word "me"
1 – 4	Toe heel right and left	Hands on hips
5 – 8	Shuffle hop step right	Hands on hips
1 – 4	Toe heel left and right	Hands on hips
5 – 8	Shuffle hop step left	Hands on hips
1 s/o 8	Repeat toe heels, shuffle hop step right and left	
1 s/o 8	Feet together move heels right, left, right, left	Hands on heart
1 – 4	Jump feet a part	Arms out to side
5 – 8	Hold	Hands point to self
		word "me"
3 s/o 8	Step right foot to side,	
	shuffle hop step left foot – 3 times	hands out to side
1 s/o 8	Feet together move heels right, left, right, left	Hands on heart
4 s/o 8	Heel side, toe back, heel side, step together	Hands on hips
1 s/o 8	Feet together move heels right, left, right, left	Hands on heart
1 – 4	Jump feet a part	Arms out to side
5 – 8	Hold	Hands point to self
		on word "me"

Line up; Share time
Walk into room

Ballet
Warm – up at the barre
- Demi plié in 1st, 2nd, and 3rd
- Grande plié in 1st
- Tendu from 1st to front, side, and back
- Rond de jambe front
- Kicks front and side

Stretching
- Straddle
- Splits right, center, and left

Across Floor
- Chaîné turns
- Step pique passé on relevé

Center
- Balancé
- Échappé
- Pas de chat
- Changement
- Soutenu

Monthly Dance – "Somewhere Over the Rainbow" by Judy Garland

Tap
Warm – up
- Toe taps front, side, and back
- Heel digs front and side
- Heel drops
- Roll ankles

Across Floor
- Flap
- Flap heel
- Flap ball change
- Heel, brush back, toe to the back, drop heel (moving backwards)

Center
- Shuffle step
- Shuffle hop step

Game – "If You're Happy and You Know It" with the parachute
Story Time

Counts	Steps	Arms
1 s/o 8	Bourrée forward	Arms in high 5th
2 s/o 8	4 piqué passé step to right	Arms in 2nd
1 - 6	Soutenu	Arms in high 5th
7 & 8	Hold	
1 s/o 8	Bourrée forward	Arms in high 5th
2 s/o 8	4 piqué passé to left	Arms in 2nd
1 – 6	Soutenu	Arms in high 5th
1 – 6	Hold	
2 s/o 8	Balancé – right, left right, left,	Arms in 4th
1 s/o 8	2 Échappé	Arms in 2nd
1 – 6	Soutenu	Arms in high 5th
7 & 8	Hold	
1 s/o 8	Bourrée backwards	Arms in high 5th
2 s/o 8	4 piqué passé to right	Arms in 2nd
1 – 6	Soutenu	Arms in high 5th
7 & 8	Hold	

Line up; Share time
Walk into room

Ballet
Warm – up at the barre
- Demi plié in 1st, 2nd, and 3rd
- Grande plié in 1st and 2nd
- Tendu from 1st to front, side, and back
- Rond de jambe front and back
- Kicks front and side

Stretching
- Straddle
- Splits right, center, and left

Across Floor
- Chaîné turns
- Step pique passé on relevé

Center
- Balancé
- Échappé
- Pas de chat
- Changement
- Soutenu

Free Dance – with ribbons

Tap
Warm – up
- Toe taps front, side, and back
- Heel digs front and side
- Heel drops
- Roll ankles

Across Floor
- Flap
- Flap heel
- Flap ball change
- Heel, brush back, toe to the back, drop heel (moving backwards)

Center
- Shuffle hop step
- Shuffle ball change

Monthly Dance – "Rock Around the Clock" by Bill Haley
Story Time

Counts	Steps	Arms
3 s/o 8	Bounces	Hands on knees
1 s/o 8	Twist	
2 s/o 8	8 steps touch side to side – start to right	Claps side to side
2 s/o 8	Shuffle ball change right 4 times	Arms out to side
1 s/o 8	4 toe heel walks around self	Arms forward with
	right, left, right, left	palms pushed up
1 s/o 8	Twist	
2 s/o 8	8 steps side to side – start to left	Claps side to side
2 s/o 8	Shuffle ball change left 4 times	Arms out to side
1 s/o 8	4 toe heel walks around self	Arms forward with
	left, right, left, right	palms pushed up
1 s/o 8	Twist	
4 s/o 8	Heel dig, brush back, toe, heel drop	Hands on hips
	(moving backwards) right and left 4 times	
2 s/o 8	Flap heel forward 8 times	Hands on hips
2 s/o 8	8 steps touch side to side – start to right	Claps side to side
2 s/o 8	Shuffle ball change right 4 times	Arms out to side
1 s/o 8	4 toe heel walks around self	Arms forward with
	right, left, right, left	palms pushed up
1 s/o 8	Twist	
2 s/o 8	8 steps side to side – start to left	Claps side to side
2 s/o 8	Shuffle ball change left 4 times	Arms out to side
1 s/o 8	4 toe heel walks around self	Arms forward with
	left, right, left, right	palms pushed up
1 s/o 8	Twist	

Line up; Share time
Walk into room

Ballet
Warm – up at the barre
- Demi plié in 1st, 2nd, and 3rd
- Grande plié in 1st and 2nd
- Tendu from 1st to front, side, and back
- Rond de jambe front and back
- Kicks front, side, and back

Stretching
- Heel stretch
- Splits right, center, and left

Across Floor
- Chaîné turns
- Piqué turns

Center
- Balancé
- Échappé
- Pas de bourrée

Monthly Dance – "Beauty and the Beast" from Disney's *Beauty and the Beast*

Tap
Warm – up
- Toe taps front, side, and back
- Heel digs front and side
- Heel drops
- Roll ankles

Across Floor
- Flap ball change
- Heel, brush back, toe to the back, drop heel (moving backwards)
- Buffalo

Center
- Shuffle hop step
- Shuffle ball change
- Stamp hop step
- Cramp roll

Game – Parachute with beanbags
Story Time

"Beauty and the Beast" from Disney's **Beauty and the Beast**

Counts	Steps	Arms
4 s/o 8	Round de jambe right, left, right, left	Arms in 2nd
1 s/o 8	Balancé right and left	Hands on hips
1 – 4	Pas de bourrée right	Hands on hips
5 – 8	Échappé	Hands on hips
1 s/o 8	Balancé right and left	Hands on hips
1 – 4	Pas de bourrée right	Hands on hips
5 – 8	Échappé	Hands on hips
1 s/o 8	Stand in 1st	Arms port de bras low 5th 1st, 2nd
1 s/o 8	Balancé left and right	Hands on hips
1 – 4	Pas de bourrée to left	Hands on hips
5 – 8	Échappé	Hands on hips
1 s/o 8	Balancé left and right	Hands on hips
1 – 4	Pas de bourrée left arms	Hands on hips
5 – 8	Échappé	Hands on hips
1 s/o 8	Stand in 1st	Arms port de bras low 5th 1st, 2nd
1 s/o 8, 1 – 4	3 piqué turns to right	Arms in 1st
5 – 8	Curtsey	Arms demi 2nd
1 s/o 8, 1 – 4	3 piqué turns to left	Arms in 1st
5 – 8	Relevé in 5th, hold	Arms in high 5th

Line up; Share time
Walk into room

Ballet
Warm – up at the barre
- Demi plié in 1ˢᵗ, 2ⁿᵈ, and 3ʳᵈ
- Grande plié in 1ˢᵗ and 2ⁿᵈ
- Tendu from 1ˢᵗ to front, side, and back
- Rond de jambe front and back
- Kicks front, side, and back

Stretching
- Heel stretch
- Splits right, center, and left

Across Floor
- Chaîné turns
- Piqué turns
- Chassé sauté in arabesque

Center
- Balancé
- Échappé
- Pas de bourrée

Free Dance – with maracas

Tap
Warm – up
- Toe taps front, side, and back
- Heel digs front and side
- Heel drops
- Roll ankles

Across Floor
- Flap ball change
- Heel, brush back, toe to the back, drop heel (moving backwards)
- Buffalo
- Step side with right, shuffle left, hop, and step crossing left over right

Center
- Shuffle hop step
- Shuffle ball change
- Stamp hop step
- Cramp roll

Monthly Dance – "I Won't Grow Up" from Disney's *Peter Pan*
Story Time

Counts	Steps	Arms
Hold till lyrics begin		
1 s/o 8	Flap ball change right and left	Hands on hips
1 s/o 8	Shuffle ball change, shuffle hop step right	Hands on hips
1 s/o 8	Flap ball change left and right	Hands on hips
1 s/o 8	Shuffle ball change, shuffle hop step left	Hands on hips
2 s/o 8	Cramp roll right to the 4 walls	
	right side, back, left side, front	Arms forward with palms pushed up
1 s/o 8	Step right, shuffle hop cross left 2 times	Arms out to side
1 – 4	Stomp right	Point to self
5 – 8	Stomp left	Point to self
1 – 4	Stomp right	Point to self
5 – 8	Stomp left	Point to self
1 s/o 8	Flap ball change right and left	Hands on hips
1 s/o 8	Shuffle ball change, shuffle hop step right	Hands on hips
1 s/o 8	Flap ball change left and right	Hands on hips
1 s/o 8	Shuffle ball change, shuffle hop step left	Hands on hips
2 s/o 8	Cramp roll right to the 4 walls	
	right side, back, left side, front	Arms forward with palms pushed up
1 s/o 8	Step right, shuffle hop cross left 2 times	Arms out to side
1 – 4	Stomp right	Point to self
5 – 8	Stomp left	Point to self
1 – 4	Stomp right	Point to self
1 – 4	Stomp	Hands on hips and nod head

Line up; Share time
Walk into room

Ballet
Warm – up at the barre
- Demi and grande plié in 1st, 2nd, and 3rd
- Tendu from 1st to front, side, and back
- Rond de jambe front and back
- Kicks front, side, and back

Stretching
- Heel stretch
- Splits right, center, and left

Across Floor
- Chaîné turns
- Piqué turns
- Chassé sauté in arabesque
- Step leap

Center
- Balancé
- Échappé
- Pas de bourrée
- Assemblé

Monthly Dance – "I See the Lights" from Disney's *Tangled*

Tap
Warm – up
- Toe taps front, side, and back
- Heel digs front and side
- Heel drops
- Roll ankles

Across Floor
- Heel, brush back, toe to the back, drop heel (moving backwards)
- Buffalo
- Maxie ford
- Step side with right, shuffle left, hop, and step crossing left over right

Center
- Shuffle ball change, shuffle hop step
- Stamp hop step
- Flap cramp roll

Game – Parachute Tag
Story Time

Counts	Steps	Arms
2 s/o 8	Hold	
1 s/o 8	Balancé right and left	Arms out to side
1 s/o 8	Pas de bourrée right and left	Arms out to side
1 s/o 8	Balancé right and left	Arms out to side
1 s/o 8	Pas de bourrée right and left	Arms out to side
1 – 4	Échappé	Hands on hips
5 – 8	Step left, assemblé right	Hands on hips
3 s/o 8	Repeat échappé, step assemblé 3 times	Hands on hips
2 s/o 8	Chassé sauté to the 4 walls	
	to right, to back, to left, to front	Arms in 4th
1 – 4	Échappé	Hands on hips
5 – 8	Step left, assemblé right	Hands on hips
3 s/o 8	Repeat échappé, step assemblé 3 times	Hands on hips
1 s/o 8	Hold relevé in 5th	Arms in high 5th
1 s/o 8	Balancé right and left	Arms out to side
1 s/o 8	Pas de bourrée right and left	Arms out to side
1 s/o 8	Balancé right and left	Arms out to side
1 s/o 8	Pas de bourrée right and left	Arms out to side

Line up; Share time
Walk into room

Ballet
Warm – up at the barre

- Demi and grande plié in 1st, 2nd, and 3rd
- Tendu from 1st to front, side, and back
- Rond de jambe front and back
- Kicks front, side, and back

Stretching

- Heel stretch
- Splits right, center, and left

Across Floor

- Chaîné turns
- Piqué turns
- Step leap

Center

- Balancé
- Échappé
- Pas de bourrée
- Assemblé
- Pirouette

Free Dance – with picture book and CD

Tap
Warm – up

- Toe taps front, side, and back
- Heel digs front and side
- Heel drops
- Roll ankles

Across Floor

- Heel, brush back, toe to the back, drop heel (moving backwards)
- Buffalo
- Maxie ford
- Step side with right, shuffle left, hop, and step crossing left over right

Center

- Shuffle ball change, shuffle hop step
- Stamp hop step flap step (time step)
- Flap cramp roll

Monthly Dance – "Wake Me Up Before You Go Go" by Wham!
Story Time

Counts	Steps	Arms
1 – 4	Stop right left	
5 – 8		2 claps
1 – 4	Stop right left	
5 – 8		2 claps
1 – 4	Stop right left	
5 – 8		2 claps
1 – 4	Stop right left	
5 – 8		2 claps
1 s/o 8	Flap ball change right and left	Hands on hips
1 s/o 8	Stomp, hop, step, flap, step	Hands on hips
1 s/o 8	Flap ball change left and right	Hands on hips
1 s/o 8	Stomp, hop, step, flap, step	Hands on hips
1 s/o 8, 1- 4	Shuffle ball change right 3 times	Hands on hips
5 – 8	Shuffle hop step	Hands on hips
1 s/o 8, 1- 4	Shuffle ball change left 3 times	Hands on hips
5 – 8	Shuffle hop step	Hands on hips
	Turn and face left	Hands on hips
28 counts	Heel, brush, heel drop, toe, heel 7 times	Hands on hips
5 -8	March left right, turning to face right	Hands on hips
28 counts	Heel, brush, heel drop, toe, heel 7 times	Hands on hips
5 – 8	March left right turning to face front	Hands on hips
2 s/o 8	Twist	
2 s/o 8	8 flap heels forward	
	Jump feet to 2nd	Arms up

Line up; Share time
Walk into room

<u>Ballet</u>
Warm – up at the barre
- Demi and grande plié in 1ˢᵗ, 2ⁿᵈ, and 3ʳᵈ
- Tendu from 1ˢᵗ to front, side, and back
- Rond de jambe front and back
- Kicks front, side, and back

Stretching
- Heel stretch
- Splits right, center, and left

Across Floor
- Chaîné turns
- Piqué turns
- Step leap

Center
- Balancé
- Échappé
- Pas de bourrée
- Assemblé
- Pirouette

Monthly Dance – "Ever Ever After" by Jordan Pruitt

<u>Tap</u>
Warm – up
- Toe taps front, side, and back
- Heel digs front and side
- Heel drops
- Roll ankles

Across Floor
- Heel, brush back, toe to the back, drop heel (moving backwards)
- Buffalo
- Maxie ford
- Step side with right, shuffle left, hop, and step crossing left over right

Center
- Shuffle ball change, shuffle hop step
- Stamp hop step flap step (time step)
- Flap cramp roll

Game – "If You're Happy and You Know It" with the parachute
Story Time

Counts	Steps	Arms
Hold till lyrics begin		
1 s/o 8	4 chaînés turns forward	Arms in 1st
1 s/o 8	Stand in 3rd/5th	Port de bras arms low 5th, 1st high 5th open to 2nd
1 – 4	Plié relevé in 3rd/5th	Arms in high 5th
5 – 8	Hold	
1 s/o 8	Balancé right and left	Arms in 2nd
1 – 4	Plié relevé in 3rd/5th	Arms in high 5th
5 – 8	Hold	
1 s/o 8	Balancé right and left	Arms in 2nd
1 – 4	2 chassé side to right	Arms out to side
5 – 8	Step left assemblé right	Arms out to side
1 – 4	2 chassé side to left	Arms out to side
5 – 8	Step right, assemblé	Arms out to side
1 – 4	Chassé forward leap	Arms out to side
5 – 7	Land in arabesque and hold	Arms in 4th
8	Close 1st facing right	Arms in 1st
2 s/o 8	4 piqué turns to back	Arms in 1st
1 – 4	Chassé forward leap	Arms out to side
5 – 7	Land in arabesque and hold	Arms in 4th
8	Close 1st and pose	Arms in 1st

Chapter Nine
Choreography Guide Lines for Recital Dances

Choreographing recital dances for young children is a formula more than a creative process. The goal is to have well presented routines, which showcase the past year. Remember, you want to make students look their best so their parents will see the end result and be happy with their child's dance experience. You also want the various dances to look different to the audience and show a progression of difficulty based on age and skill level.

The formula for creating these dances is based on repetition. For young dancers, it works best to pick out a song that fits the pattern of: verse, chorus, verse, chorus, verse, chorus. For the Petite A level, you want every verse to have the same choreography and every chorus to have the same choreography. This gives you the outline of ABABAB (A is the verse and B is the chorus). For Petite B, pick out a song that contains the musical pattern of: verse, chorus, bridge, verse, chorus. Again the verses and choruses should have the same choreography, but the bridge creates a slightly more complex formula of ABCAB. Finally, for Petite C you should make each verse (or bridge) have different choreography, but keep the chorus the same, which gives you the formula of ABCBDB. Below are additional guidelines to use with the formula.

Petite A: 1 – 1 ½ minutes

- Walk on and off stage with assistance; no specific line-up order
- Start all in 1 straight line, center stage; no opening pose
- No formation changes
- No walking/dancing backwards or upstage
- No choreography facing the back of the stage
- Use repeats in choreography as much as possible (ABABAB)
- Follow teacher's hand gestures/directions
- Stand and bow together with direction

Petite B: 1 – 1 ½ minutes

- Walk on and off stage with assistance; no line-up order
- Start all in 1 straight line, center stage; know opening pose
- 1 formation change
- No walking/dancing backwards or upstage
- No choreography facing the back of the stage
- Change levels in dance, i.e.: kneeling or sitting
- Use repeats in choreography as much as possible (ABCABCAB)
- Follow teacher's hand gestures/directions
- Stand and bow together with little direction

Petite C: 1 – 1 ½ minutes

- Specific line-up order; remember it on own
- Walk on and off stage without assistance
- Start all in 1 straight line, center stage; know opening pose
- 2 - 3 formation changes
- Change levels in dance, i.e.: kneeling or sitting
- Use repeats in choreography (ABCBDB)
- Know dance with little cues from teacher
- Know ending pose; able to stand and bow together without direction

By following these simple formulas and guidelines, you will have successful and stress-free dances for your younger students. This will allow you to focus your creative process on students with a stronger dance base.

Chapter Ten

Games

Directional Songs

The following directional songs can be found on many different children's CD's, by various artists. The song tells the various motions to do while you listen and follow along with your students.

> *"The Hokey Pokey"*
>
> *"Head, Shoulders, Knees and Toes"*
>
> *"London Bridge is Falling Down"*
>
> *"Left and Right Machine--The Robot Song"*
>
> *"I'm Going on a Bear Hunt"*

Games

Mother, May I?

The leader gives directions to the group or an individual child. The child or group must ask, "Mother, may I?" before moving. The leader then replies, "Yes, you may," before the child can complete the direction. If a child does not ask, "Mother may I," and/or if the leader says, "No, you may not," the players stay where they are. Vary the game by adding different dance movements; for example, the directions could be to do 3 chassés, or 3 bourrées. The game ends when everyone is over the finish line and seated.

Monkey Say, Monkey Do

Have the children stand or sit in a circle. Give instructions to the children and give them a chance to do it. For example, "Monkey says, 'Touch your nose…Scratch your stomach…Eat a banana…Peel a banana,'" or anything else a monkey might do. The "monkey" (or leader) should say and demonstrate what they want to do, and the other children should imitate it.

Red Light, Green Light

Have the children line up at one end of the room. The leader stands at the other end of the room and turns their back to the other children. When the leader says, "Green light," the children walk toward the leader. When the leader says, "Red light," the children must stop. As soon as the leader says red light, he/she turns around to catch any child still moving. Any children caught still walking are sent back to the starting line. If the children are very young, just call out the names of the ones still moving and try again.

Twister Two

This is a simple variation on the Twister board game. Use primary colored place markers or a parachute. Call out a body part and a color, and children should put that body part on that color, such as, "Finger on blue," then, "Foot on yellow." Depending on the coordination of the group, you can leave the finger on blue while they try to put a foot on yellow, or children can return to their original places before the second move is called.

Front and Back

Children stand behind a line on the floor. The leader calls, "Front," and children jump over the line. When the leader yells, "Back," children jump backwards over line. If the children are in front and the leader calls front, they do not move. A variation on this game is *In the Water*. It is the same idea, but each child has a hula-hoop, which is the water. The leader calls, "In the water," and children jump in the hoop. When the leader calls, "Out of the water," the children jump out of the hoop. You can play to win by having children who move when they should not sit out, and play till there is one child left.

Sticky Popcorn

Explain to the children that they are going to pretend to be pieces of very sticky popcorn in a popper. The children will pop around the room until they bump into someone. If they touch someone, they are stuck together and must pop together. The children pop until the whole group is stuck together. You will need to demonstrate this game, but once they understand it, the game goes really fast. You can play a variation of tag in which one child is "it" and tries to get stuck to the other children while they try to stay away.

"Miss Gina" Says

This is played just like the game *Simon Says*, but you use your own name instead. Remember to use dance terms, because this is a great game for testing children to see if they know the names of different dance steps.

Kangaroo Hop

Students start at one side of the room. Have them place a beanbag or beanie animal between their knees. Students try to jump all the way across the room.

Parachute Games

Parachute Tag

Lift the parachute high overhead. Call one child's name and have him or her run (or skip, hop, twirl, crawl, etc.) to the other side before the parachute comes down and tags them.

Parachute with Beanbags

Throw a few beanbags on top of the parachute, and see if you can get them to stay on while moving the parachute. Next, try to get them off as fast as you can.

"If You're Happy and You Know It" with Parachute

Sing the directional song, "If You're Happy and You Know It," but add in directions you can do with the parachute, such as: up and down, side to side, shake, etc.

Free Dance

The *free dance* involves a variety of props, improvisation, and music. Guide them by giving visuals as well as different types of music, then have them dance as to how it makes them feel. For the free dance with picture book and CD, find a picture book from any famous Ballet and the music for that specific ballet. Show the students a picture and play a song. Have the students dance as if they were in the costume or playing the role from the photo you showed them. The *free dance* is students' favorite part of class, since they get to move around freely and exercise their individual creativity. Remember do not let this turn into students running around in circles for 3 minutes.

Supplies and Music

Supplies for Class

Scarves

Place-markers in different shapes and/or colors

Small balance beam

Hula-hoops

Small tunnel

Maracas

Ribbons

Mini trampoline

Beanbags

Parachute

Small plastic cones

Tumbling mat

Small stuffed animals

Jingle bells on circular elastic band for wrist and/or ankles

Music for Monthly Dances

"Swinging on a Star" by Bing Crosby

"You've Got a Friend in Me" by Randy Newman

"Good Ship Lollipop" by Shirley Temple

"Never Fully Dressed" from the musical *Annie*

"A Dream is a Wish Your Heart Makes" from Disney's *Cinderella*

"Singin' in the Rain" by Gene Kelly

"Part of Your World" from Disney's *The Little Mermaid*

"Rainbow Connection" from *The Muppets*

"Wind Beneath My Wings" by Bette Midler

"Tomorrow" from the musical *Annie*

"At the Hop" by Danny and the Juniors

"Locomotion" by Grand Funk Railroad

"When You Wish Upon a Star" from Disney's *Pinocchio*

"Rockin' Robin" by Bobby Day

"When Will My Life Begin" from Disney's *Tangled*

"I'm So Excited" by The Pointer Sisters

"Let's Go Fly A Kite" from Disney's *Mary Poppins*

"Stupid Cupid" by Connie Francis

"Somewhere Over the Rainbow" by Judy Garland

"Rock Around the Clock" by Bill Haley

"Beauty and the Beast" from Disney's *Beauty and the Beast*

"I Won't Grow Up" from Disney's *Peter Pan*

"I See the Light" from Disney's *Tangled*

"Wake Me Up Before You Go-Go" by Wham!

"Ever Ever After" by Jordan Pruitt